Animal Alphabetizing

Find the word that comes between the two words alphabetically.

1. **llama** and **lynx**
2. **cardinal** and **chipmunk**
3. **baboon** and **buffalo**
4. **flamingo** and **frog**
5. **elephant** and **emu**
6. **monitor** and **mouse**
7. **leopard** and **lizard**
8. **calf** and **cat**
9. **mockingbird** and **monkey**
10. **eagle** and **elephant**
11. **bulldog** and **buzzard**
12. **falcon** and **finch**

Look at the first letter in each word. Is it the same? If so, look at the second letter. If it's the same, look at the third letter.

Answer Box

A	B	C	D	E	F
lobster	fox	cheetah	moose	mole	badger
G	H	I	J	K	L
egret	lion	camel	ferret	burro	elk

Objective: Use knowledge of alphabetizing to order words; practice research and study skills.

1

Top Guide Words

Read the dictionary entries.

black • blouse `4`

black \ blak\ *adj.* the darkest of all colors; the opposite of white

blossom \ blä´səm\ *n.* the flower of a plant or tree

bighorn • bite `3`

bighorn \ big´hôrn´\ *n.* a wild sheep that lives in the Rocky Mountains

birthmark \ bûrth´märk´\ *n.* a mark on the body that was there at birth

below • bicycle `2`

below \ bē lō´\ *prep.* in a lower place, beneath

beverage \ bev´ər ij\ *n.* a liquid for drinking such as milk or juice

baby • belly `1`

baby \ bā´ bē\ *n.* a very young child

backpack \ bak pak\ *n.* a large sack for carrying supplies on the back

baker \ ba´ kər\ *n.* a person whose work is making foods such as bread, cake and cookies

ball \ bôl\ *n.* any round body or sphere

barber \ bär´ bər\ *n.* a person whose work includes giving haircuts and shaves

beach \ bēch\ *n.* the sloping shore of a body of water

beanstalk \ bēn stôck\ *n.* the main stem of a bean plant

beaver \ bē´vər\ *n.* a large rodent that lives on land or water and has soft, brown fur and broad, flat tail

bedbug \ bed´ bug\ *n.* a small insect that bites and can get into beds

begin \ bē gin´\ *n.* to do the first part of something, make a start

Guide words are found at the top of each dictionary page. The first guide word tell what word comes first on the page. The second guide word tells what word comes last.

Use the dictionary pages to answer the questions about guide words.

1 Between which two guide words is the word ball found?

2 Between which two guide words is the word blend found?

3 Between which two guide words is the word bird found?

4 Between which two guide words is the word belt found?

5 What is the first word you would find on page 1?

6 What is the last word you would find on page 4?

7 What is the first word you would find on page 2?

8 What is the last word you would find on page 3?

9 What word is found between the guide words below and bicycle?

10 What word is found between the guide words black and blouse?

11 What word is found between the guide words baby and belly?

12 What word is found between the guide words bighorn and bite?

> Remember, the guide words at the top of each dictionary page can help you locate words.

Answer Box

A	B	C	D	E	F
bighorn and bite	beverage	below and bicycle	baby and belly	blouse	black and blouse

G	H	I	J	K	L
baby	bedbug	below	blossom	birthmark	bite

Objective: Recognize the purpose of guide words; locate
words in a dictionary, using guide words.

3

Dictionary Word Hunt

Read the definitions below.

bulky • burlap

bulky \ bul´ kē \ *adj.* big and awkward

bull \ bool\ *n.* an adult male cattle, buffalo, elephant, moose, or whale

bulldog \ bool´ dōg\ *n.* a short, stout dog with powerful jaw

bullfrog \ bool´ frôg\ *n.* a type of large, loud frog

bulwark \ bul´ wark\ *n.* a solid wall-like structure raised for defense

bumble \ bum´ bəl\ *v.* to do clumsily

bumblebee \ bum´ bəl bi\ *n.* a large, round bee covered in black and yellow fuzz

bump \ bomp\ *v.* to jolt or knock something

bumpkin \ bump´ kin\ *n.* an awkward, clumsy person

bundle \ bun´ dəl\ *n.* a number of things tied or wrapped together

bungalow \ bung´gə lō\ *n.* a small house

bunny \ bun´ə\ *n.* a rabbit

bunt \ bunt\ *v.* to bat softly

buoy \ boo ē\ *n.* a special floating device used to mark a water hazard

buoyant \ boi´ ənt\ *adj.* able to float

burger \ bər´gər \ *n.* a short form of hamburger-style sandwiches

bureau \ byoor´ō\ *n.* chest of drawers

burglar \ bûr´glər\ *n.* a thief

burlap \ bûr´lap\ *n.* a rough fabric

You can use a dictionary to find out the meaning of words you don't know.

Find the words that complete the sentences.

1 The sack that carried the grain was made of ▦.

2 The boy was a ▦ the way he bumped into things and knocked them over.

3 The large package was ▦ and awkward to carry.

4 The woman carried her ▦ home from the store.

5 The strong, thick wall served as a ▦ against the enemy.

6 The ▦ climbed through the window and stole all of the jewelry and money from the house.

7 The coach told the baseball player to ▦ instead of hitting the ball as hard as he could.

8 Floating in the harbor, the ▦ signals ships to beware of the shallow water.

9 The awkward girl seemed to ▦ everything she tried to do.

10 The young couple lived in a little ▦ by the sea.

11 Mother folded the clothes and placed them neatly in the ▦.

12 The boat the boy made was ▦.

Answer Box

A	B	C	D	E	F
buoyant	bumpkin	bulwark	bumble	bunt	burlap

G	H	I	J	K	L
burglar	buoy	bulky	bureau	bundle	bungalow

Objective: Recognize the purpose of a dictionary; determine the meanings of unknown words, using dictionary definitions and context.

Volumes of Letters

Find the encyclopedia number that has information beginning with each letter shown.

AB	CD	EF	GHI	JK	LM	NO	PQ	RS	TU	VW	XYZ
1	2	3	4	5	6	7	8	9	10	11	12

> Each encyclopedia has subjects that begin with a certain letter. You can see the letters on the outside of each encyclopedia volume.

1 the letter N

2 the letter X

3 the letter H

4 the letter Q

5 the letter T

6 the letter W

7 the letter A

8 the letter K

9 the letter E

10 the letter D

11 the letter S

12 the letter M

Answer Box

A	B	C	D	E	F
Volume 1	Volume 2	Volume 3	Volume 4	Volume 5	Volume 6

G	H	I	J	K	L
Volume 7	Volume 8	Volume 9	Volume 10	Volume 11	Volume 12

Objective: Identify the volume number of an encyclopedia that corresponds to a particular letter; use alphabetizing skills.

Encyclopedia Hunt

Find the encyclopedia volume where you would find information for each subject.

1 the Grand Canyon

2 the Colorado River

3 Thomas Jefferson

4 the Empire State Building

5 the republic of Zaire

6 the Boston Tea Party

7 the Taj Mahal

8 the state of New Hampshire

9 Abraham Lincoln

10 the state of Rhode Island

11 the Wright Brothers' first flight

12 the city of Quebec

Information in an encyclopedia is arranged in alphabetical order by subject.

Answer Box

A	B	C	D	E	F
AB 1	CD 2	EF 3	GHI 4	JK 5	LM 6

G	H	I	J	K	L
NO 7	PQ 8	RS 9	TU 10	VW 11	XYZ 12

Objective: Identify the encyclopedia volume in which information can be found; use alphabetizing skills.

7

Outline Ins and Outs

Read the article on elephants. Note information in the article that you might use in a report about kinds of elephants and their bodies.

Elephants

Elephants are the largest land animals. A full-grown male elephant may weigh as much as 14,000 pounds and grow to be 10 feet tall. Elephants spend about 16 hours a day eating. They eat roots, grasses, leaves, tree branches, and bark. They can eat as much as 300 to 600 pounds of food a day and drink as much as 30 to 40 gallons of water.

An elephant's trunk has more than 40,000 muscles. The elephant uses its trunk for many things. It uses its trunk to drink and to bathe. An elephant also uses its trunk like an arm and a hand. It uses its long trunk to reach leaves and strip bark. It can pick up things that weigh 600 pounds. It can also pick up things as small as a peanut. The elephant uses its trunk like a nose for breathing and smelling. It uses its trunk to communicate and to embrace and greet other elephants. It even uses its trunk to spank its young.

There are two kinds of elephants—African and Asian. African elephants are taller and more slender. They live in grassy plains. The Asian elephants are shorter. They live in dense forests. One way to tell African elephants from Asian elephants is by their ears. The ears of the African elephant are larger and rounded. The ears of the Asian elephant are smaller and more triangular.

Elephants live in herds made of families. They help each other take care of the young. Baby elephants are called calves. They grow about 20 months inside a mother elephant before they are born. They weigh between 180 and 250 pounds at birth and stand about 3 feet tall.

> Be sure the information you note relates to your purpose for reading.

Now find the <u>main idea</u> and <u>supporting details</u>.
Organize the information in the outline.

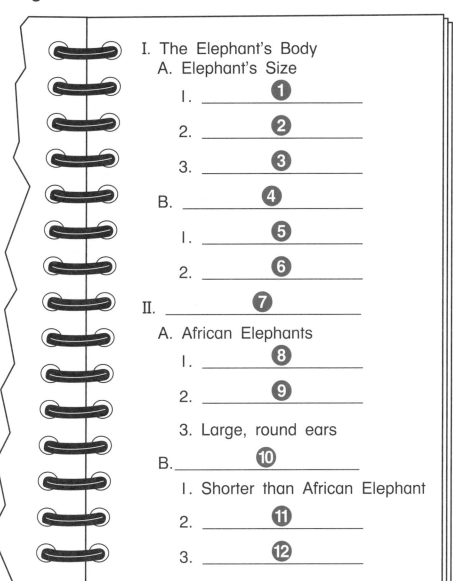

I. The Elephant's Body
  A. Elephant's Size
    1. _____ ① _____
    2. _____ ② _____
    3. _____ ③ _____
  B. _____ ④ _____
    1. _____ ⑤ _____
    2. _____ ⑥ _____

II. _____ ⑦ _____
  A. African Elephants
    1. _____ ⑧ _____
    2. _____ ⑨ _____
    3. Large, round ears
  B. _____ ⑩ _____
    1. Shorter than African Elephant
    2. _____ ⑪ _____
    3. _____ ⑫ _____

An outline presents information in the same order as the longer version.

Answer Box

A	B	C	D	E	F
Elephant's Trunk	Asian Elephant	Small, triangular ears	Tall and slender	Used to drink and bathe	Lives in grassy plains
G	**H**	**I**	**J**	**K**	**L**
Kinds of Elephants	Largest land animal	14,000 pounds	Used to pick up things	10 feet tall	Lives in dense forests

Objective: Read for relevant information in a nonfiction expository article; organize main ideas and supporting details in an outline.

Library Book Search

All nonfiction books in the library are organized by the **Dewey Decimal System**. All books in a category have the same numbers. These numbers are called **call numbers**. All libraries organize the books using call numbers so books can be found easily.

Study the chart that shows how books are organized.

Dewey Decimal System

000–099	**General Reference**		500–599	**Science**
030	Encyclopedias		510	Mathematics
070	News Media		520	Astronomy
090	Rare Books		550	Earth Sciences
100–199	**Philosophy**		600–699	**Technology**
130	Paranormal Phenomena		610	Medicine
150	Psychology		690	Buildings
200–299	**Religion**		700–799	**Fine Arts**
220	Bible		740	Drawing
280	Christian Denominations		780	Music
290	Other Religions		790	Drama
300–399	**Social Studies**		800–899	**Literature**
340	Law		810	American Literature
370	School		840	French Literature
390	Customs		870	Latin Literature
400–499	**Languages**		900–999	**History—Travel**
420	English		910	Geography
460	Spanish		930	History of Ancient World

Use the information in the chart to answer the questions.

1 What is the subject of a book with the call number 780?

2 What call number would you look for to find books about schools?

3 What call number would you look for to find books about math?

4 What is the subject of a book with a call number between 200 and 299?

5 What call number would you look for to find encyclopedias?

6 What call number would you look for to find a book about drawing?

7 What call numbers would you look for to find a book about earthquakes?

8 What is the subject of a book with the call number 910?

9 What call numbers would you look for to find books about maps?

10 What is the subject of a book with the call number 610?

11 What is the subject of a book with the call number 790?

12 What call numbers would you look for to find books about languages?

The Dewey Decimal System can help you find a book about a certain subject.

Answer Box

A	B	C	D	E	F
drama	510	music	religion	370	400–499

G	H	I	J	K	L
900–999	030	550	medicine	geography	740

Objective: Recognize the purpose of the Dewey Decimal System; identify call numbers and subject areas using the Dewey Decimal System.

11

A Title Page

Read the title pages. Answer the questions.

1 Who is the author of *How to Play Football*?

2 What book did B. Beard write?

3 In what state can you find the Scales Publishing company?

4 Who wrote the book about reptiles?

5 What book did Ima Quarterback write?

6 What author had his book published in Salem, Massachusetts?

7 In what city is Crossbones Publishing located?

8 What book did Liz R. Tayle write?

9 What publishing company is located in Salem, Massachusetts?

10 What publishing company published a book by Liz R. Tayle?

11 Who published *How to Play Football*?

12 In what state did Ms. Quarterback have her book published?

The Adventure on Pirate Island

B. Beard

Crossbones Publishing
Salem, Massachusetts

How to Play Football

Ima Quarterback

Pigskin Publishing
Goal Post, Florida

Reptiles

Liz R. Tayle

Scales Publishing
Phoenix, Arizona

Answer Box

A	B	C	D	E	F
Crossbones Publishing	Arizona	The Adventure on Pirate Island	B. Beard	Ima Quarterback	Liz R. Tayle
G	**H**	**I**	**J**	**K**	**L**
How to Play Football	Pigskin Publishing	Florida	Reptiles	Salem, Massachu-setts	Scales Publishing

Objective: Locate title, author, publisher, and other information on a title page.

A Table of Contents

Read each Table of Contents. Answer the questions.

1 On what page would you begin reading about the rules of football?

2 On what page would you begin reading about lizards?

3 In which chapter could you find out about snapping turtles?

4 In which chapter could you find out about the equipment needed to play football?

5 On what page would you begin reading about crocodiles?

6 On what page would you begin reading about the special training a quarterback needs?

7 In which chapter could you find out information about the rattlesnake?

8 In which chapter could you find out the names of the football teams?

9 On what page would you begin reading to find out how to care for a pet snake?

10 On what page would you begin reading about football fans?

11 In what chapter would you find out how many points a touchdown scores?

12 On what page would you find out about what reptiles eat?

How to Play Football

Contents

Reptiles

Contents

Answer Box

A	B	C	D	E	F
page 4	Teams	page 20	Scoring	Snakes	page 30
G	**H**	**I**	**J**	**K**	**L**
page 12	page 9	page 8	Turtles and Tortoises	page 1	Equipment

Objective: Locate information using a Table of Contents page; practice research skills.

13

An Index

Study the index from a book about reptiles.

INDEX

A
alligator, 1, 5, 6, 20–23

B
boa constrictor, 9
bones, 2

C
camouflage, 3
chameleon, 13
classification, 1–3
cobra, 10
crocodile, 1, 5, 6, 20–23

DE
domeshell tortoise, 17
eggs, 5
enemies, 7
eyes, 3

FG
food, 4
gecko, 14
grass snake, 9

HIJ
habitat, 6–7
hatching, 5
horned lizard, 12
iguana, 13

KL
king cobra, 10
Komodo dragon, 12
lizard, 12–15

MN
mating, 3
mongoose, 7
monitor lizard, 13

OP
poisonous snakes, 8, 10
python, 10

QR
rattlesnake, 10
reproduction, 5

S
salamander, 14
sand viper, 10
scales, 1, 14
senses, 3
skeleton, 2
skin, 1
snake, 8–11
survival, 7–8

TUV
tail, 12,18
teeth, 2, 4, 22
temperature, 3
tortoise, 16–19
turtle, 16–19
vertebrae, 2
viper, 10

WXYZ
whiptail lizard, 13

Find the number of the page or pages where you can learn information about each topic.

1. geckos

2. food for reptiles

3. vipers

4. bones of reptiles

5. whiptail lizard

6. turtles

7. hatching reptiles from eggs

8. scales of reptiles

9. survival of reptiles

10. camouflage

11. boa constrictor

12. Komodo dragons

Look at the first letter in each word. Then use that letter to help look up the word in the index.

Answer Box

A	B	C	D	E	F
pages 16–19	pages 1 and 14	page 2	page 3	page 10	page 9
G	**H**	**I**	**J**	**K**	**L**
page 12	page 4	page 5	page 14	page 13	pages 7–8

Objective: Identify pages on which information can be found, using an index; practice research skills.

15

A Glossary

A **glossary** is a special dictionary at the end of a book that is used to help you understand the meaning of words in the book. This is a glossary from a book about airplanes.

Read the glossary from a book about airplanes.

GLOSSARY

A

Air lanes Common routes for airplanes.

Aviator A pilot. Someone who operates an airplane.

C

Compressor blades Parts of a jet engine that press together the air before it is mixed with fuel.

E

Engine mount A metal frame that attaches the engine to the airplane.

F

Fuselage The body of the aircraft.

G

Glider An aircraft that does not have an engine.

P

Pitch The up-and-down motion of the nose of a moving airplane.

Propeller A device made up of blades.

Pusher prop A propeller that pushes an airplane along.

R

Roll The motion of an airplane rocking from side to side.

T

Tail Assembly The rear section of an aircraft.

Y

Yaw A swinging motion of an aircraft around its axis.

Use the glossary to fill in the blanks.

1. The ⬜ flew the plane from Boston to Chicago.

2. A device made up of blades is the ⬜.

3. A ⬜ presses together the air before it mixes with fuel.

4. The body of the aircraft is the ⬜.

5. The rudder, fins, and elevators are found at the rear of the airplane, also known as the ⬜.

6. Airplanes keep to their ⬜ to help avoid mid-air crashes.

7. The ⬜ moves the airplane along by pushing the plane.

8. The swinging motion of an aircraft around its center line is the ⬜.

9. The pilot controlled the ⬜ of the airplane to keep it from rocking too much to either side.

10. The metal frame that attaches the engine to the airplane is the ⬜.

11. The aircraft that flies without an engine is a ⬜.

12. As the nose of the airplane moved up and down, the pilot adjusted the ⬜.

> Remember that a glossary is arranged in alphabetical order.

Answer Box

A	B	C	D	E	F
engine mount	pusher prop	glider	tail assembly	yaw	pitch

G	H	I	J	K	L
aviator	fuselage	roll	compressor blade	propeller	air lanes

Objective: Recognize the purpose of a glossary; identify word meaning using a glossary; practice research and study skills.

17

A Thesaurus

Read the thesaurus entries.

bite		**walk**

bite *(v.)* To crush with the teeth.
I bite carefully into the juicy peach.

chew   To crush slowly with the teeth.
Always *chew* your food slowly.

nibble   To bite in a quick, gentle way.
Rabbits *nibble* on the lettuce in our garden.

cook *(v.)* To prepare food with heat.
You cook pasta before you eat it.

bake   To cook in an oven.
We *bake* lasagna in the oven.

grill   To cook on a metal rack over heat. We will *grill* hamburgers and hot dogs at the park today.

steam   To cook in the hot mist that rises from boiling water. We *steam* vegetables and seafood.

get *(v.)* To look for and bring back.
Please get the newspaper for me.

buy   To trade money for something.
I will *buy* the toy for five dollars.

purchase   To buy. We will collect money and *purchase* a get-well gift for our teacher.

put *(v.)* To set, to lay, or to place.
The class members all put their names on the card.

place   To put. Do not *place* the newspapers near the fireplace.

spread   To distribute over a surface. Good painters *spread* the paint evenly as they work.

sprinkle   To scatter in small amounts. *Sprinkle* coconut over the muffins.

say *(v.)* To pronounce or to speak.
They say the lines of the play perfectly.

declare   To say openly and strongly. We *declare* our independence from England.

describe   To tell about. Please *describe* what you saw on your vacation.

discuss   To talk over. My parents *discuss* the news every night.

explain   To make plain. The teacher will *explain* the math problem.

proclaim   To make known. The team members *proclaim* their victory.

shout   To say something in a loud voice. We *shout* when our team wins.

speak   To say words; to talk. I will *speak* with the teacher before class.

talk   To speak. They *talk* with one another politely.

tell   To say in words. The campers *tell* stories around the campfire.

whisper   To speak softly. I *whisper* in the library.

walk *(v.)* To go on foot.
We walk to the store to get exercise.

march   To walk with even steps. The drummers *march* in the band.

move   To change position or place. I will *move* to the next table.

step   To move by walking. We *step* in time to the music.

stroll   To walk in a slow, easy way. People *stroll* through the park on Sunday.

Read the story. Find the best vivid verb to take the place of each underlined word.

After School

After school, when Megan and Michael **1** <u>walk</u> along the street, they often stop to look in the store windows. At the pizza parlor, they watch as the chef prepares the pizza. First the chef rolls out the dough, and then she **2** <u>puts</u> tomato sauce all over it. Next she **3** <u>puts</u> cheese on top of the sauce. Finally she **4** <u>cooks</u> the pizza. Megan goes into the pizza parlor and **5** <u>gets</u> a slice. She takes the slice and tries to **6** <u>bite</u> the crust, but it is too hot.

A little further along the street, the children meet a man who **7** <u>cooks</u> hot dogs on a charcoal fire. The hot dogs smell delicious, and Michael asks, "How much will it cost to **8** <u>get</u> one of those?" Michael puts mustard and relish on the hot dog and **9** <u>bites</u> it slowly as they continue their walk home.

Suddenly the children hear some music and turn to look as a band **10** <u>walks</u> by. The leader **11** <u>says</u>, "Halt," and then the band begins to play. Megan **12** <u>says</u>, "I love this music!" As the band continues down the street, the children follow along, eating their snacks and keeping time to the music.

> A **thesaurus** can help you make your writing interesting. Notice how each word helps you picture the action in a different way.

Answer Box

A	B	C	D	E	F
purchases	shouts	declares	buy	grills	marches

G	H	I	J	K	L
sprinkles	chews	spreads	nibble	bakes	stroll

Objective: Recognize the purpose of a thesaurus; replace bland words with vivid words, using a thesaurus; practice a writing strategy.

A Chart

Look at the chart that shows different kinds of plant-eating animals.

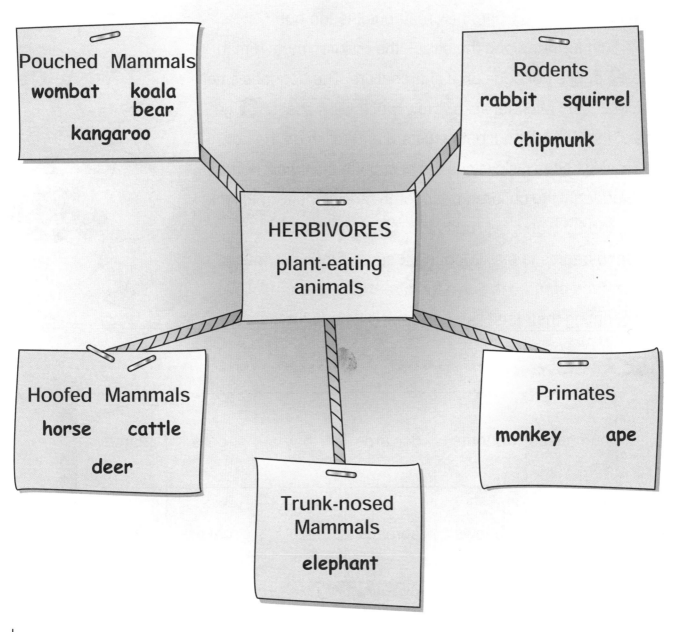

20

Use the chart to answer the questions.

1 What does this chart show?

2 How many groups of mammals are shown on the chart?

3 To which group of mammals do rabbits belong?

4 To which group of mammals do cattle belong?

5 To which group of mammals do wombats belong?

6 How many animals are shown in the Rodents group?

7 How many animals are shown in the Primates group?

8 Which group of mammals only has one member listed?

9 Which animal belongs to the Primates group?

10 Which animal belongs to the Hoofed Mammals group?

11 Which animal belongs to the Rodents group?

12 Which animal belongs to the Pouched Mammals group?

You can find different animal groups on the chart. Each group has examples.

Answer Box

A Pouched Mammals	B monkey	C cattle	D two	E three	F Trunk-nosed Mammals
G Rodents	H squirrel	I Hoofed Mammals	J Herbivores	K koala bear	L five

Objective: Recognize the purpose of a chart; interpret a chart to answer questions; practice research and study skills.

21

A Schedule

Read the TV schedule.

SATURDAY NIGHT

	6:00	6:30	7:00	7:30	8:00	8:30	9:00	9:30
2	News Hour		Home Movies	Funniest Kids	Ask the Experts		Movie Night "Monster Scare"	
5	News	Movie Review	Funny Papers	Neighbors	You Bet! Game Show	Think About It Game Show	Your Health	Cook With Me
7	News	An Interview with The President		All in a Day	Silly Animals	Family Time	At the Movies "My World"	
11	Children's Hour		All About Dinosaurs		In the Wild		At the Opera	
22	Baseball ⟶					Sports News		Highlights

SUNDAY NIGHT

	6:00	6:30	7:00	7:30	8:00	8:30	9:00	9:30
2	News Hour		Family Fun Hour		Clowning Around	TV Court	Outdoor World	On the Road
5	News	Music Today	In the News	In the Kitchen	You Bet! Game Show	Magic with Mr. E		
7	News	Where Are They Now?		All in a Day	Silly Animals	Family Time	At the Movies "Speedy"	
11	Children's Hour		Kid's Night at the Movies "Clowns on Parade"				News "Around Town"	
22	Baseball ⟶					Sports News		Golf Highlights

Read across the top of the schedule to find the times.

Use the schedule to answer the questions.

1 What game show can you watch on both Saturday and Sunday night on Channel 5?

2 On what channel can you watch baseball both Saturday and Sunday night?

3 What show can you watch on Saturday night if you wanted to learn how to make tacos?

4 What is on Channel 7 at 7:30 on Sunday night?

5 On what channel can you watch "An Interview with the President" at 6:30?

6 When can you watch "Home Movies"?

7 How long is the show "All about Dinosaurs"?

8 When can you watch "Golf Highlights"?

9 How long is the movie "Clowns on Parade"?

10 When can you watch "Music Today"?

11 How long is the game show "Think About It"?

12 On what channel can you watch "Outdoor World" on Sunday night?

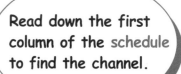

Read down the first column of the schedule to find the channel.

A	B	C	D	E	F
two hours	Channel 7	Channel 2	Sunday at 9:30	You Bet!	one hour
G	**H**	**I**	**J**	**K**	**L**
half an hour	Cook with Me	Channel 22	Saturday at 7:00	Sunday at 6:30	All in a Day

Objective: Recognize the purpose of a schedule; interpret information in a television schedule; practice research skills.

A Diagram

Study the diagram of the human digestive system.

The Digestive System

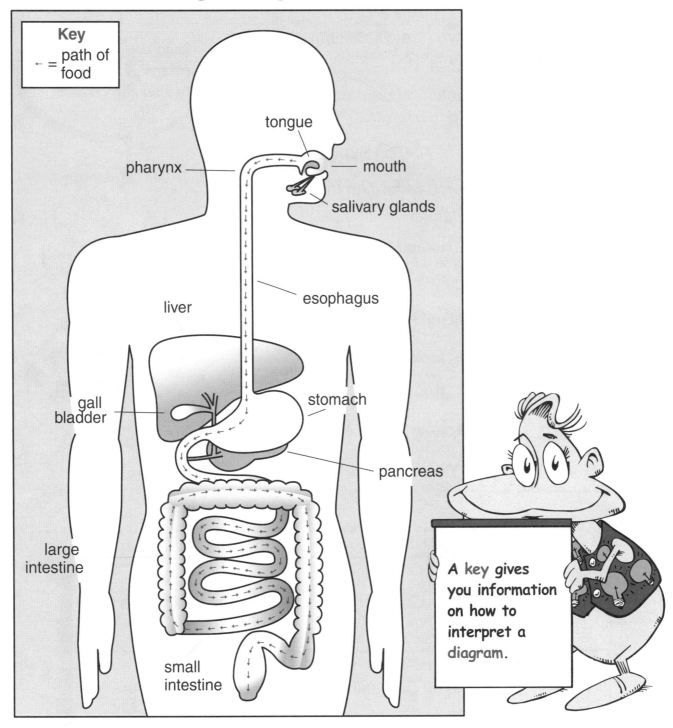

Key
← = path of food

tongue

pharynx

mouth

salivary glands

esophagus

liver

gall bladder

stomach

pancreas

large intestine

small intestine

A key gives you information on how to interpret a diagram.

Use the diagram to answer the questions.

1. This diagram shows the ■.

2. Digestion begins in the ■, where teeth and saliva start to break up food.

3. The ■ is the tube that carries food from the mouth to the stomach.

4. Food does not pass through the ■, the largest organ in the body.

5. Food passes from the esophagus to the ■ where it continues to digest.

6. From the stomach, the food passes into the ■.

7. The little pouch beneath the liver is called the ■.

8. Another name for the throat is the ■.

9. The ■ is between the liver and the large intestine and behind the stomach.

10. From the small intestine the food passes into the ■.

11. The ■ is found inside the mouth.

12. The ■ are found beneath the tongue.

Answer Box

A	B	C	D	E	F
salivary glands	pharynx	esophagus	pancreas	gall bladder	large intestine
G	**H**	**I**	**J**	**K**	**L**
mouth	small intestine	tongue	stomach	digestive system	liver

Objective: Recognize the purpose of a diagram; interpret a diagram using callouts; practice research and study skills.

25

A Bar Graph

Study the bar graph.

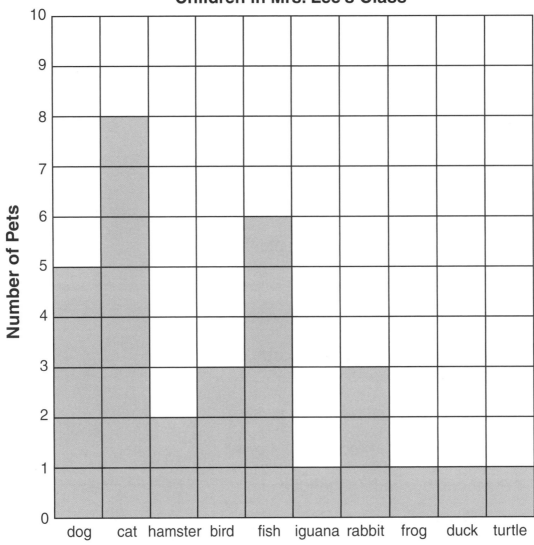

Number of Pets Owned by the Children in Mrs. Lee's Class

(Number of Pets vs. Kinds of Pets: dog, cat, hamster, bird, fish, iguana, rabbit, frog, duck, turtle)

Three spaces above rabbit are shaded. That tells you that three rabbits are owned by the children in Mrs. Lee's Class.

Use the graph to answer the questions.

1 How many birds are owned by the children in Mrs. Lee's class?

2 What kind of pet is the most common?

3 How many iguanas are owned by the children?

4 Mrs. Lee's class has the same number of birds as it does of which other pet?

5 How many more cats than fish are owned?

6 What is the second most common pet owned by the children of Mrs. Lee's class?

7 Mrs. Lee's class owns only two of which pet?

8 Besides an iguana, a frog, and a turtle, what pet does only one child own?

9 Are there more dogs or rabbits owned?

10 How many more cats than rabbits are owned by the children?

11 How many fish do the children own?

12 How many more dogs than iguanas are owned by the children?

Answer Box

A	B	C	D	E	F
fish	cat	five	hamster	one	dogs

G	H	I	J	K	L
four	duck	three	rabbit	two	six

Objective: Recognize the purpose of bar graphs; interpret a graph to answer questions; practice research and study skills.

An Atlas

Look at the map.

The United States of America

You can use the **compass rose** to find north, south, east, and west.

Key
★ = state capital

Use the map to answer the questions.

1 What does this map show?

2 What does a star symbol mean?

3 What state on this map is the farthest east?

4 What is the largest state along the Pacific Ocean on this map?

5 What state is along the north border of New Mexico?

6 What is the capital of Illinois?

7 What state would you first enter traveling east from Kansas?

8 In which direction would you travel to go from Colorado to Utah?

9 What is the body of water south of Louisiana called?

10 What is the capital of Arkansas?

11 In which direction would you travel to go from Alabama to Georgia?

12 What is the body of water east of North Carolina called?

Answer Box ·

A	B	C	D	E	F
Missouri	Little Rock	Colorado	east	Atlantic Ocean	west
G California	**H** The United States	**I** Maine	**J** Gulf of Mexico	**K** Springfield	**L** state capital

Objective: Recognize the purpose of a map; interpret a U.S. map to answer questions; practice research and study skills.

29

A Map

Look at the map.

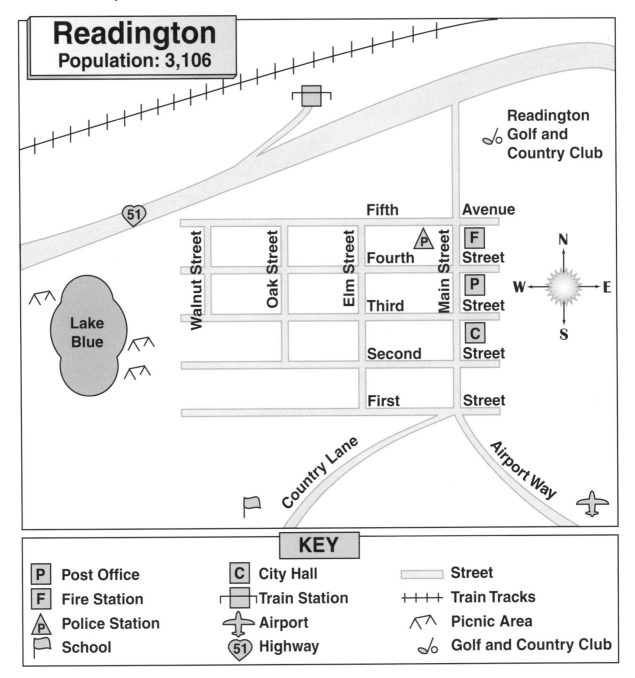

Readington
Population: 3,106

Readington Golf and Country Club

Fifth Avenue

Walnut Street

Oak Street

Elm Street

Main Street

Fourth Street

Third Street

Second Street

First Street

Lake Blue

Country Lane

Airport Way

N
W   E
S

KEY

P	Post Office	C	City Hall		Street
F	Fire Station		Train Station	++++	Train Tracks
P	Police Station		Airport	⌃⌃	Picnic Area
	School	51	Highway		Golf and Country Club

Use the map to answer the questions.

1 What does this map show?

2 What is the first street west of Main Street?

3 What is the symbol for the train station?

4 What building is on the other side of Main Street from the Fire Station?

5 Where can you find picnic areas?

6 Airport Way becomes what street as it enters into town?

7 What is the symbol for train tracks?

8 What does P stand for?

9 In what direction would you need to travel to get from First Street to Fifth Avenue?

10 Lake Blue is in what direction from town?

11 What is the symbol for a school?

12 What highway runs through Readington?

Remember to use the map key to help you read the map.

Answer Box

A	B	C	D	E	F
Police Station	west	Post Office	(51)	Lake Blue	north

G	H	I	J	K	L
++++	Readington	Main Street	Elm Street	⊞	⚑

Objective: Interpret a map key and compass rose to answer questions about a map; practice research and study skills.

Symbol Sense

Match each sign with its meaning.

① 　　② 　　③

④ 　　⑤ 　　⑥

⑦ 　　⑧ 　　⑨

⑩ 　　⑪ 　　⑫

Look at the details in each sign. Think about what the picture might stand for.

Answer Box

A	B	C	D	E	F
two-way traffic	playground	women's restroom	no trucks	traffic signal	parking
G	**H**	**I**	**J**	**K**	**L**
telephone	place to sleep	men's restroom	place to eat	airport	deer crossing

Objective: Interpret graphical signs that convey information related to community places and travel.